Praise for Ch...

How to Stay Single Forever

"HOW TO STAY SINGLE FOREVER is a must read for every woman engaged in the eternal search for Mr. Right now."
—**Lynn Harris, author of** *He Loved Me, He Loves Me Not: A Guide to Fudge, Fury, Free Time, and Life Beyond the Breakup*

"A punchy antidote to every relationship specialist shrieking 'we'd better hurry up and buy a puppy and start walking it around the local basketball courts or prowl salad bars ready to give out friendly nutritional advice if we don't want to end up spinsters (at 28!).' Jenny reminds us that we can do quite well thank-you-very-much without some big lug hanging around."
—**Sarah B. Weir, general editor,** *Double X: A User's Guide*

"With great tips like 'have too many cats,' 'be a stalker,' and 'get religion,' Jenny has given straight women all over America a fighting chance for singledom. HOW TO STAY SINGLE FOREVER is a helpful guide to avoiding the pitfalls of devoting your life to a guy who will do you nothing but dirt."
—**Liz Tracey, author of** *So You Want to Be a Lesbian*

How to Stay SINGLE Forever

JENNY LOMBARD

WARNER BOOKS

A Time Warner Company

Warner Books, Inc., 1271 Avenue of the Americas,
New York, NY 10020
Visit our Web site at
http://pathfinder. com/twep

W A Time Warner Company

Printed in the United States of America
First Printing: February 1997
10 9 8 7 6 5 4 3 2 1

LIBRARY OF CONGRESS CATALOGING-IN-PUBLICATION DATA
Lombard, Jenny.
    How to stay single forever / Jenny Lombard.
        p.   cm.
    ISBN 0–446–67194–0
    1. Single women—humor. 2. dating (Social customs)—Humor.
3. Man-woman relationships—Humor.   I. Title.
PN6231.S5485L66 1997
818´.5402—dc20   96–16775
                                          CIP

Book design and text composition by Kathryn Parise
Cover design and illustration by Lou Brooks

To my husband and five children . . .

just kidding!

Acknowledgments

Many people contributed their humor and experience to this undertaking. Of those, I would especially like to thank Michael Horowitz (an expert in his own right), the E.S.T. Playwrights Unit, Peter Pope, Peter and Peggy Anne Lombard, Peggy Watson, and my agent, Victoria Sanders. Finally, this book could not have happened without the support of my editor, Diane Stockwell.

Introduction

Why not admit it? Despite the plethora of social forces that would have you feel otherwise, the possibility of eternal singledom intrigues you. Well, it's nothing to be ashamed of. After all, except for multiple births and airplane crashes, most of us enter and exit this world in a state of singleness. In terms of art, power, and achievement, history has taught us that it is single people who get ahead, not couples. Think about the women who have made the greatest contribution to society in the last five hundred years. Catherine the Great, Joan of Arc, Emily Dickinson, Dorothy Parker, Ivana Trump—the list goes on, and all of them, technically speaking, were single. And if you're still not convinced of the benefits of remaining single, then perhaps you should ask yourself: What is the alternative to singleness?

Whether you are in one, looking for one, or trying to leave one behind, everyone knows relationships are hard. Getting to know someone is no piece of cake. It requires trust and vulnerability—the likelihood that one or the other of you will get hurt is very high. But this book is not about your personal horror story, nor is it an attempt to convince you that singledom is the answer for you. It is, merely, what it promises to be: a compilation of the 101 best ways to remain single forever.

Remember: There are no easy answers. Behavior that may guarantee one woman a lifetime unhampered by relationships may prove to be the fatal blow that drives another straight into the arms of a loving and devoted spouse. If one technique doesn't work for you ("Become a Thrill Seeker," for instance), you may want to try another (Fetishes? Cults? Dating actors?). Allow yourself to explore. Mixing and matching is perfectly acceptable. How about a life in the arts (#2) with a dash of tactlessness (#35) thrown in for good measure? Or a masochistic disposition with a fixation on unavailable, alcoholic partners? Get creative. Don't be afraid to experiment until you find the right combination for you. With a little patience, you too can have a life unencumbered by significant romantic involvements!

Author's note: There are a few methods that I have avoided including, for reasons of good taste and sensitivity. While disfigurement may be a relatively cheap and easy way of remaining single forever, it gives one an unfair advantage over the rest of us. Acts of violence and bloodshed, too, have been consciously avoided. Many radical singles will regard this as a cop-out but I believe part of the great challenge of remaining single forever is to do so without resorting to artificial means.

How to Stay

SINGLE

Forever

Only Sleep with Men Who Are More Screwed Up Than You Are

If there is a cardinal rule of single dating, this would have to be it. "But if it were as easy as all that," you may well ask, "wouldn't everyone be single?"

Unfortunately it is almost impossible to determine in advance who will be the crazier partner in a love affair. The reason why is that sanity, within the context of a relationship, is entirely a matter of chemistry. There is, however, one surefire method that can help you predict which one of you will be the looser cannon. When you meet a man you find attractive, observe his behavior and ask yourself the following questions:

Are his personal grooming habits excessive in any way; for example, does he bathe compulsively, or not at all?

Does he have prolonged depressions followed by periods where he is very high?

Does he carry on conversations with people who are not there?

Does he rock back and forth when he's concentrating?

If you answered yes to any of these, and you're still interested in him, then there's no doubt about it. You're crazier than he is.

2

Go into the Arts

While choosing a career in the arts may not ensure a life of single-dom, it is definitely a step in the right direction. The Sisyphean task of trying to support yourself while pursuing your dreams requires a single-mindedness that does not leave much room, emotionally speaking, for the demands of a relationship. Furthermore, the less successful you are in your chosen field, the more likely it is that you will eventually become a bitter, jaded harpy with a precarious sense of self. Therefore, I suggest devoting your life to an art form toward which the world at large is totally indifferent. Clogging? Fire dancing? Raku pottery? The possibilities are endless.

There are, however, exceptions to every rule. If one day over a cappuccino, you find yourself making eye contact with a scruffy-looking guy in a black leather jacket, my advice is to get the check and get out of there as fast as you can. He may be a poet whose blackly comic paeans to his belly button have been rejected by every publishing house in the country. The two of you have a lot in common.

3

Live in a City

Psychologists have observed that in test groups overcrowding elicits very specific reactions in the social behavior of certain mammals. Aggressive, territorial behavior becomes prevalent, the rate of female ovulation increases, and there is a marked increase in homoerotic behavior in both the male and the female of the species. When mating does occur it is rarely long-term. Fertility in viable males decreases. Not only that but in certain extreme cases of overcrowding, mothers are twelve times as likely to eat their own young.

And if you think we're bad, you should see what it does to the rats.

4

Don't Lower Your Standards

Setting a standard for what is acceptable in a lover and never wavering from it is a great way to protect yourself from the mind-bending challenges of intimacy. Therefore, if your lover has a weak chin, poor table manners, and hasn't read *A Confederacy of Dunces* by John Kennedy Toole you will never have to look beyond these superficial flaws to notice he is also kind, loving, and absolutely crazy about you.

5

Have a Few Skeletons in the Closet

If you had a troubled childhood it's always a good idea to share your traumatic experiences with your lover in great detail. This is most effective when you have just slept with someone for the first time, and your partner is feeling vulnerable. When you light up that post-coital cigarette and launch into your tale of scary childhood abuse and incest, it'll make him think twice about what the word "baggage" is all about.

A word of warning—this approach might actually work against you if he's the caretaking type, or if you met in a twelve-step program.

6

Be Hard Up

In the Victorian era, long periods of celibacy were regarded as signs of moral strength in the face of temptation. Today it just means that you're screwed up. We all have our dry periods but only someone who is truly committed to staying single will let her partner know just how long it's been since her last act of coitus, particularly if the lag time is now stretching into the double digits (I'm talking years, not months). So if your itch hasn't been scratched since the days of Jordache jeans and disco bags, go ahead, let him know!

7

Date an Actor

As every woman in New York or Los Angeles knows, dating actors is one of the best ways to ensure that you stay single forever. Actors only have one true love: themselves. They are their stars and their moon, they are their sunrise and sunset, and this love of theirs never disappoints them—unless, of course, they don't get the job, in which case you'll witness more head-banging than at a Woody Woodpecker film festival. Since many actors are not lacking in personal charms they are to the single woman what the catnip mouse is to the kitten.

A word of warning: Some of them have been known to stick like glue to other theatrically minded people such as agents or casting directors. If you are one of these or can help their careers in any other way it's best to avoid them entirely.

8

Have a Fetish

One successful single woman I know finds the sight of a man eating a hard-boiled egg deeply erotic. Another can only achieve orgasm while encased entirely in rubber. But saddest and loneliest of all is "Lorna," who claims that she feels a sexual thrill every time Newt Gingrich takes the House floor on C-SPAN. Her tortured fantasy world is so sick she can't meet my gaze as she tries to put into words the whirl of emotions inside her: "Newt . . . spank me . . . in bunny slippers."

The sicker and more specific your fetish the less likely it is that you will ever find a partner who is willing to indulge it—but good luck anyway, Lorna. I'm looking forward to reading about that one in the *Washington Post*.

9

Never Resist a Punch Line

One A.M., Saturday night, his place. The music is soft, the lighting is flattering. You emerge from the bathroom in a dramatic satin negligee. Wordlessly, he unknots his bow tie and flings it carelessly across the room toward a priceless Louis XIV bed. Mother-of-pearl button by mother-of-pearl button, he undoes his tuxedo shirt and makes his way toward you, desire blazing in his deep-set green eyes. As he gathers you into his arms he murmurs the words that a thousand women in a hundred different countries would thrill to hear . . . "Ma chére, speak to me. Tell me what is in your heart."

"Is that a banana in your pocket or are you just happy to see me?" may not be the response he is expecting, but it will ensure that you stay single forever.

10

Bounce a Rebounder

If a man has just broken off a nine-year relationship, chances are moving in with you and your three kids was not what he meant when he told his ex-wife he needed to see other people. Keep forcing the issue. See where it gets you.

//

Only Go Out with Guys Who Have Money

Your doting grandmother may have told you that you deserved the best, but if you are missing your two front teeth, weigh in at three hundred pounds, and have been working in a ball-bearing factory for the last eleven years, chances are Donald Trump may not be dying to meet you. But don't worry—if only champagne, caviar, and roses can turn your head then you'll have plenty of reason to spurn the guy who's standing next to you on the assembly line. He's been dying to buy you a Genessee for the last decade.

12

Too Many Cats

For most women, there's a thin line between being a desirably quirky companion and being a bitter old hag. Having too many cats is one way of signaling to a man that you have crossed that line. "But how many cats is too many?" you may ask nervously as little Weegee and Oscar mewl in the background. Well, it's not quantity so much as quality. Three tidy little Siamese kittens won't do much to harm a woman's reputation, particularly if she's under thirty and very cute.

On the other hand, if you're pushing forty and have a cat that weighs eighteen pounds, sheds on your winter clothes, and urinates on the furniture, one cat is probably way too many for most men to handle.

13

Date Younger Men

As a feminist, I wish I could tell you that the liberated notion of sleeping with men more than ten years younger than you is a good idea. Unfortunately, grim reality has taught me otherwise. While there is certainly no dearth of men who prefer mature women to their own peers, age differences between two people pose many problems, none of which can be overcome easily. No matter how open your mind is, dating younger men remains a predictably efficient way to stay single forever.

But don't take my word for it. Why not consult an expert: your mother. After all, what do you think she's been doing down in Florida now that your father's gone?

14

Date Older Men

Another excellent means of remaining single forever is by dating older men. The reason why is that older men have grown up in an earlier era and have a completely different set of expectations when it comes to sex and romance. Rather than simply wanting a torrid affair, the older man may want to grab as much joy as he can from life by getting married.

And that's why you should never have left your nice octogenarian millionaire boyfriend alone for two minutes with his seventeen-year-old nurse!

15

Date Men Your Own Age

Developmentally speaking, females mature at different rates than males. For instance, when a girl is seventeen, most of the boys in her age group show only the emotional growth of a fourteen-year-old. When that girl is a woman of thirty, naturally the men in her age group will also have matured. Most of them will then be fourteen and a half (see #13).

16

Have a Long-Distance Romance

As we have seen, it is possible to achieve eternal singledom through the careful cultivation of relationships with unavailable men. In the lexicon of these "nonrelationships," nothing bears fruit quite so fruitlessly as the Long-Distance Romance. In the LDR, as it is known in some quarters, the single woman becomes emotionally attached to a partner in another hemisphere, so that she can remain unavailable in her own.

Unfortunately, due to the incredible popularity of frequent flyer programs, the LDR is not what it used to be. Just to be on the safe side, I advise choosing lovers from inaccessible, war-ravaged countries that are in the midst of incredible upheaval—Chechnya, Bosnia, or East L.A.

17

Don't Flirt

Statistics indicate that in certain colonies of the *Picoides arcticus* (the Arctic three-toed woodpecker), natural selection seems to favor females who flash their tail feathers over those who build the sturdiest nests. Several continents away, in western Africa, those female putty-nosed monkeys who groom the alpha male are impregnated 60 percent more frequently than those who mind their own business. And in dog runs on the West Side of Manhattan, it has been observed that boy dogs are twice as likely to mount a yapping little schnauzer than a standoffish Irish setter.

So if you don't want anyone splashing in your gene pool, refuse to flirt with the male of your species. Not only won't you have any fun, but you may well stay single forever!

18

Mention Children

When W. C. Fields was asked how he liked children his reply was "parboiled." From the number of Barney toys and Super Soakers on the market we can only assume that not all men feel this way. On the other hand, not every woman whose biological clock is ticking is desperate to have a child. Where do you stand on the subject?

That's a good question to bring up to get the conversational ball rolling on a first date, don't you think?

19

Use Baby Talk in Bed

A woman who gurgles and punctuates her lovemaking with the words "Dada" and "Mama" can make a disconcerting sex partner. Unless he's Humbert Humbert, this kind of behavior is guaranteed to give most men a major case of the willies and will help you remain single forever.

On the other hand, if after trying this technique he becomes enflamed and starts referring to you as "Daddy's little girl," call 1-800-777-TIPS. The operators at America's Most Wanted are standing by.

20

Bring Mom Along

When you first met, you both agreed that you didn't want to rush into anything. On your first date you parted with a big goodbye hug. On your second date you moved on to a chaste good-night kiss. The third date there was more kissing—but less chasteness. Now you're getting ready for your fourth date. It's eight o'clock and you know that five minutes after he rings your doorbell you're both going to be lying on the floor of your foyer, stark naked, in a pool of each other's sweat. What to do?

Don't worry. The answer is right there on your speed dial. Your mother. Call her up, invite her over, tell her there's a nice young man you want her to meet. I guarantee she'll take it from there.

21

Make Like a Tree and Leave

Hopping a freight train at daybreak with all your belongings stuffed in a cardboard suitcase may seem like a draconian method of remaining single, but in some cases it may be the only thing that works. On a smaller scale, tiptoeing out of his bedroom at four A.M. with your clothes in your arms also gets the message across loud and clear: *Noli me tangere,* buddy.

22

Need to Be Needy

One woman I know swears that her habit of leaving twenty consecutive messages on a man's answering machine is the secret to her eighteen relationship-free years. Another friend promises that clinging and begging him not to leave you works wonders—especially if you're out on a date and he's only trying to visit the men's room. There's no doubt about it—as a means of staying single forever nothing sends 'em running for the hills like a good dose of female neediness.

Then again, you may not have to work that hard. Sometimes the words "I had a nice time. When will I see you again?" may be all it takes. After all, neediness is in the eye of the beholder.

23

Go Online

While you may indeed strike up a conversation with someone intelligent on the Internet, keep in mind that most of the men you will meet there tend to spend large chunks of their time in darkened rooms, downloading film clips of Sharon Stone onto their hard drive, and posting messages with *Star Trek* bulletin boards.

Of course there are exceptions to every rule. After all, Rush Limbaugh met his wife online. And if that's not a reason to stay off the Information Superhighway and single forever, I don't know what is!

24

Embrace the Double Standard

Despite the fact that women have had the vote for fifty years, in-formal surveys indicate that many female doctoral candidates feel deeply insecure about the fact that their closest friends from high school have six kids and are living in a mobile home when all they have to show for themselves is a Ph.D. in genetic engineering from MIT. If you pursue a career in science or technology while contin-uing to buy into the theory that "a woman's place is in the trailer park" not only will you develop facial tics and a tendency to work fifteen-hour days, but you will eventually become so insecure that you may stay single forever.

Every cloud has a silver lining, however; only a woman who's a failure in the eyes of the world could find a cure for cancer.

25

Tell Him You're a Virgin

Let's face it, in this age of instant gratification, there's something a little perverse about people who refuse to satisfy their deepest needs. Therefore, if you want to raise the stakes of a sexual encounter from casual to spookily surreal, I suggest you tell your lover that you're a virgin. This is especially effective if you're over thirty or you picked each other up just minutes before.

As for the fact that you enjoyed the favors of half of your high school football team—what he doesn't know won't hurt him. Remember, women have been lying about their virginity for centuries!

26

Be a Nervous Nelly

Since so much of Nervous Nellyism has to do with behavior, we have assembled the following list of verbal and nonverbal cues favored by the terminally agitated. Practice these behaviors regularly (especially on first dates) and you too can achieve a state of perpetual singledom.

1. Compulsive shredding of table linens over dinner.
2. Nervous tics, sweaty forehead, armpit stains.
3. Jumpy: flinching every time the waiter approaches.
4. Quivering, shaky hands, rattling tea cup.
5. High-pitched, giddy laughter that goes on much too long.
6. Garrulousness, frequent use of the pronoun "I."
7. Stammering, breathlessness, a tendency to repeat oneself.

27

Join a Cult

While joining a cult will indeed limit your dating possibilities in the world at large, it will open up a whole dangerous new world of intracult dating. Not only will the other cult members become your closest friends after your brainwashing, but the cult's failed-rock-star-cum-charismatic-leader will begin to figure largely in your dreams. If you don't watch out you may end up stockpiling ammo for the bunker with a steady beau. One option for remaining single in such an environment is to join a celibate, all-female cult such as Weight Watchers or Jenny Craig.

28

Answer a Personal Ad

Put down that paper right now: Despite rumors to the contrary there is roughly a one in 10,478,687 chance that you will ever have a relationship with someone you meet through a personal ad.

On the other hand, the odds that you will win the $10 million Lotto jackpot are currently only 7 million to one. So the next time you consider spending six dollars on a coffee date with a "quirkily attractive SWM, 38, some hair" ask yourself where you would rather improve your odds.

29

Place a Personal Ad

Of the seventy-five single men that responded to your personal ad there will only be ten that you genuinely want to meet. Of those ten, six will reveal over coffee that they recently ended a marriage. Out of the remaining four suitors, one will be a reformed Mormon with adult children, one will order six beers with brunch, and something about the third's false teeth will put you off. The last fellow will be as smart as he is gorgeous. You will spend an idyllic day in the park with him talking about books but he won't return your call. Then, a month later, you'll be perusing the classifieds when you'll come across an ad that describes him to a T.

C'est la vie.

30

Date Marrieds

Dating married men is a time-honored means of staying single forever. Few people realize, however, that it also offers the single woman valuable on-the-job training for a new career: psychotherapist. As in a therapeutic relationship, the mistress is first a shoulder to cry on, then a mirror through which the married man can see himself, and finally a weekly expense he feels too guilty about to cut back on.

Please note: When a married man is talking about his problems, you, not he, should assume the reclining posture of the analysand. Listening to him in any other position will eventually cut off the flow of oxygen to your brain.

31

Choose the Restaurant

Power is a complicated thing, and for every couple interpersonal dynamics of a relationship are different. Sometimes it's clear from the beginning that the man will call the shots; in other relationships it's the woman. Sometimes the balance of power is off-kilter and needs to be adjusted. And sometimes you just want to avoid the subject completely by staying single forever.

One good way of doing that is by vetoing his choice of restaurant in favor of that fabulous new all-you-can-eat Hungarian place you've heard so much about. Not only will your bossiness immediately violate the power structure of a first date, but as an added bonus you'll always be associated with heartburn.

32

Seek Out James Bond

Ever since you saw the film *Thunderball* when you were eight (you sneaked in with your older brother), you have always longed for a man who could unzip a dress like 007. Despite years of therapy, you still believe that the men you date should own a tuxedo, sip gin martinis (stirred, not shaken), and make you murmur "Oh, James" when you're between the sheets. Well, don't give up, girlfriend. I'm sure Mr. Bond is right around the corner.

33

Get Fixated

Obsessing about every move your partner makes is, in some cases anyway, a good way of ensuring that you will remain single forever. Like the shy woodland animal who fears the sight of humankind, some experts believe that proximity to female neuroses is biologically predetermined in our species to make males flare their nostrils and stamp around skittishly on their tiny hooves. Men will do their best to distance themselves from female nuttiness—unless of course they are alcoholics, in which case they might appreciate the attention, and may even mistake it for love.

34

Don't Sober Up

It's said in recovery circles that until substance abusers admit their powerlessness over their drug of choice, they remain, emotionally speaking, the same age as when they first picked up the drug. Addictions are smoke screens that keep us isolated, not only from other people, but from ourselves. You're probably afraid of intimacy—or are you just anesthetizing yourself so you won't have to face your own pain? Did you have a lousy childhood? Did you come from an alcoholic home? Were you abused physically? What about psychologically? Until you put down that drug or that drink, you'll never work out these feelings. You'll never really know another person, or yourself. Bottom line is that all your relationships are going to be about the bottle, or the pills, or the . . .

What's that you say? I'm harshing your mellow? Sorry. Toke?

35

Be Tactless

There's nothing like a little tactlessness to get a date off on the right foot, and the sooner you establish this precedent the better chance you have of remaining single forever. Don't be shy—speak your mind, no matter how brutal your opinions may be. Some good icebreakers are:

Wow. That's some nose.
Is that supposed to be funny?
Anybody ever tell you that you st-st-st-stutter?
So tell me, how do you feel about those acne scars?

A word to the wise: If you employ this tactic on a first date, make sure you carry cash. You may get stuck with the bill.

36

Never Get Over X

Consider the story of Ronda. Her ex-boyfriend Brad was everything she wanted in a man—until the night of the junior prom when he dumped her for the large-breasted Nancy Wecker. Despite the heartbreak, Ronda still carried a torch for Brad. One evening after a big fight with her current boyfriend about why she persisted in comparing him to someone she had gone out with twenty years before, Ronda was returning home. Lost in reminiscences about her fabulous lost love, she stepped off the curb without looking both ways, and died instantly when she was struck by a Peter Pan bus.

The moral of the story is: Carrying a torch for an old lover is not only extremely off-putting to men, it can also be dangerous to your health!

37

Swim Against the Current

There's nothing like a little dose of unavailability to light a fire under a girl's butt and really make her *work* to deserve the love she can't have. If he's only ever been in relationships with very tall women of African-American descent, the fact that you're the first albino dwarf to come along may not be what's getting in the way of your happiness together. But when he says you're not his type, don't let that stop you. Keep working until he's eating out of your hand—that's when you'll discover you have nothing in common and you want to dump him anyway.

38

Just Say No to Blind Dates

If you are an intelligent and attractive single woman no doubt you have many caring friends who can't believe that you are still unattached. It is inevitable that these friends will want to set you up with their old college buddy/quirky co-worker/boyfriend's friend. No matter how unappealing he sounds, DO NOT, I repeat, DO NOT GO ON BLIND DATES! The fact of the matter is, you are seven hundred times more likely to hit it off with someone your friends pick out for you than when left to your own devices.

39

Have a Body Image Problem

BILL: You're sexy.

GINA: My thighs are way too fat.

BILL: I think your thighs are cute.

GINA: Then you think cellulite is cute.

BILL: Okay, so go on a diet if you're unhappy.

GINA: A diet? You really think I'm fat?

BILL: I didn't mean that. I just meant . . .

Repeat ad infinitum.

40

Contract a Disease

Being up-front about your sexual health is also a good way to remain single, particularly if you've ever had anything contagious. While beginning a conversation with the words "God, these cold sores are killing me" will definitely get the point across, there are also more subtle ways of broaching the subject of your STDs. Next time he's over for a drink, try leaving a bottle of Kwell out in the open—the coffee table is as good a place as any.

41

Have a Prejudice

You are deeply committed to the idea of the world as a global village and are gladly working toward the realization of this enlightened goal. You appreciate cultural diversity and have contributed to every minority organization from the Oglala Sioux Community College Support Fund to the Democratic National Committee. Your political correctitude is such that, were you standing in the Mojave Desert in your Birkenstocks at high noon, you would cast no shadow.

No matter what your good deeds are, however, persistent use of the phrase "you people" when dating someone whose otherness differs from your own will ruin your chances as an equal opportunity lover.

42

Attend a Singles Event

For some women the change is sudden. For others it's a more gradual thing. One thing's for certain, however, the longer you stay single, the more likely it is that one day you'll become desperate enough to attend a "singles event." Well don't worry—today's singles events are a lot more than soggy hors d'oeuvres and awkward conversation. If you try to keep an open mind, you're going to meet a lot of interesting, accomplished single people whom you'll want to keep in touch with . . . and they will all be women. The men, if there are any, will fulfill all your negative expectations by falling into one of two categories—the socially maladjusted geek or the over-the-hill prowler.

So go ahead, have another deviled egg. You may not meet the man of your dreams, but two weeks from now you'll have plenty of coffee dates.

43

Never Eschew the One-Night Stand

Unfortunately, we live in a time of AIDS and random violence. Brief, anonymous sexual liaisons are not what they used to be. So just to be on the safe side, the next time you're feeling frisky, instead of the usual pickup lines you might try asking:

Have you had all your shots?
Haven't I seen you somewhere before—a wanted poster?
Now, about your disease . . .

If you want to whistle a happy tune as you make your way down the winding road of perpetual singledom, don't be afraid to say: Make mine a one-nighter!

44

Have Very Smelly Feet

As any woman who's ever dated a rodeo rider knows, a fixation with Western types was not the only reason you begged him to leave his boots on during sex. Like most people raised in our antiseptic society, you probably find the odor of sweaty, snakeskin-encased feet to be a big turnoff. While it is a more common problem among men than women, your body is also capable of producing the kind of alienating stench that curdled your stomach all those years ago. In fact, all you really need is a pair of sneakers, a gym membership, and a dream.

45

Be Anorexic

Despite the fact that sex burns up as much as eighty calories an hour, most anorexics are not successful in intimate relationships. The reason why is because bingeing behavior, starvation diets, and diuretic abuse severely limit sexual desire. That's right: When asked to choose between an undressed salad or an undressed anorexic, nine hundred and ninety-nine men out of a thousand chose the undressed salad.

As for the guy who likes anorexics, he won't want to sleep with you either. He will, however, immediately book you a one-way ticket to Milan. Your bone structure is going to do wonders for his fall line . . .

46

Take No Chances

Nothing ventured, nothing gained goes the saying and if you never go to parties, never talk to men at laundromats, never force your phone number on strangers, never let yourself get hit on in bars, never flirt with people you may not like, never talk to men on line at the supermarket, never sleep with the odd loser, never let your friends arrange blind dates for you, and never answer personal ads you may, if you're very lucky, remain single forever.

47

Only Sleep with People You Don't Like

As a means of remaining unattached while still having an active sex life, never underestimate the logic of sleeping with people whom you don't particularly like. For one thing, a good dose of hostility can really set off fireworks between a man and a woman, sexually speaking. For another, if you think your lover is a heinous jerk, you probably won't want to bear his children.

Be forewarned though: Falling in love with people you don't like is something else entirely. When this happens it's usually called "marriage."

48

Have a Female Problem

Almost without exception, every prehistoric society from Outer Mongolia to Peru produced female fertility fetishes as part of its religious life. With their swollen breasts and exaggerated bellies, these wonderful artifacts are evidence that for early man the female body was a source of wonder and fear.

If you want to see a modern-day version of the same wonder and fear, try describing your yeast infection to someone you've recently started sleeping with. It won't make him want to kill a bison, but you may have a hard time getting him out of that sports bar.

49

Talk About Your Period

While we're on the subject of gynecology, it's always a great idea to
let the men you date know exactly where you are in your menstrual
cycle. Contrary to what you might believe, most men will want to
know if you have cramps or are retaining water. That way they can
time their breakup with you so as to avoid a PMS-induced scene.

50

Be Intelligent

For every man who appreciates a woman who can parse a sentence and knows the value of pi, there are two who don't. Seek them out, fall in love with them, try to have relationships with them, but whatever you do don't give up your interest in paleoclimatology. You're going to need a hobby to fall back on when it doesn't work out.

51

Be "Frigid"

Don't worry: It isn't catching. In fact, according to the *American Registry of Psychiatric Disorders*, frigidity may not even exist. What does exist, however, is the *term* "frigid." In its most common usage, this term will be applied to you by a man who is angry at you for one of two reasons: 1) He made a pass at you that you did not respond to; or, 2) He made a pass at you that you did respond to, only to discover that you have no sexual chemistry whatsoever. If a man uses this adjective to describe you, then as far as he is concerned, you will stay single forever.

52

Wear a Bathing Suit with a Skirt

While we do advise creativity in remaining single forever, it is possible to go overboard. In our opinion, one way of doing that is by wearing a bathing suit with a skirt. The wearer of the skirted bathing suit is basically making an announcement to the world that she has no sexual identity at all; it is tantamount to throwing one's beach towel into the ring of singledom.

Nevertheless, if you insist on going where no woman in her right mind would dare to go, make sure you are properly accessorized—with a string of rosary beads and your wimple.

53

Be a Stalker

Stalkers are usually confused people with some pretty big issues outside of their obsessive interest in David Letterman, Wayne Newton, and Kathie Lee Gifford. Nevertheless, in terms of staying single forever, we feel we should point out that stalkers rarely get asked out—unless it's by a bodyguard at a Madonna concert.

54

Put Him on a Pedestal

One good way of alienating a man you are dating is by putting him on a pedestal. This is especially effective if he has self-esteem problems and has never been on one before. Like anyone else, men want to be accepted for who they are. A man who rifles through your pocketbook in the middle of the night would probably be more comfortable being seen as a thief and a drug addict than the supreme master of the universe. By stubbornly refusing to acknowledge his bad qualities, you are precluding the possibility of any real intimacy occurring between the two of you.

Apropos of nothing—do you really think that joint checking account was a good idea?

55

Talk About Therapy

The single woman is like an onion. There are many layers of her identity that must be peeled in the search for self-knowledge. Only someone truly committed to living life alone, however, will insist on peeling those layers on a first date. To put it in Freudian terms, many men have a subconscious fear of hearing you talk about your Electra complex. Not only that but your therapist's jokes, when taken out of context, do not translate well.

A word of warning: If you are a therapy-head who is committed to remaining single, you should never, under any circumstances, try to pick up the tortured-looking guy in your shrink's waiting room. When his mother issues meet your father issues they're going to have a field day.

56

Be a Therapist

While many jobs are more conducive to singledom than others, few professions ensure a relationship-free future like a career as a therapist. True, Joe Sensitive will "really be able to let down his guard with you." Unfortunately, he will also pay you by the hour. As for Joe Insensitive, once he hears what you do for a living, he'll be so threatened that he won't be able to meet your gaze and will only speak to you in monosyllables. In fact, just about the only man who won't be threatened by your choice of career is another therapist.

If you should meet one of these, remember, as a medical professional you have a moral responsibility to stay single forever. Children from two-shrink marriages are always psychotic.

57

Come On Like Gangbusters

Not only do women who come on like gangbusters have more fun, but they often remain single while doing so. Because so many men still cling to the notion that "good girls don't," the woman who comes on too strong will rarely be seen as the kind of mate a man wants to bring home to mother—particularly if she has a tendency to say outrageous things in public and wears Spandex pants.

Please note: Before embarking on a career as a sexual aggressor, it's advisable to enroll in a course in assertiveness training. Rejection can be hard to take when you're lying naked across the hood of someone's car.

58

Join a Gay Gym

Your friend Martha found her husband on a Stairmaster. Babs met her last two boyfriends doing aerobics. But you're about ready to hang up your thong for good. You've been on this damned Butt-Blaster every day for the last three weeks and none of these great-looking single guys has so much as given you the time of day. If you didn't know better from the way they're checking each other out and singing along to the latest RuPaul song, it would almost make you think that they were . . . Oh, wait a second.

Come to think of it, you always were the slowest one in class.

59

Wait for Him to Make the First Move

Despite the fact that most men are taught to believe that they must be the aggressors in romantic relationships, like everyone else they are afraid of rejection. For this reason, most men require some form of female encouragement before they will make the first move. If swinging your girdle around your head while yelling "Come and git me" jars with your sense of decorum, don't worry—he'll get his nerve up one of these days. As long as you don't mind waiting . . . and waiting . . . and waiting . . . and waiting . . .

60

Make the First Move

While making the first move on a man seems like an admirably liberated romantic strategy, it often backfires. By making a pass at a man you are effectively taking the power out of his hands—something that many men will claim to appreciate but really don't. The fact that the relationship began under your initiative will eventually be nothing more than further proof of your unbearable bossiness.

What can I say? All roads lead to eternal singledom.

61

Go to Graduate School

Returning to graduate school after a long absence not only enhances one's opportunities on the job market but it can also greatly increase your chances for eternal singledom. The trick lies in pursuing a careful course of study, e.g., a degree in midwifery, elementary education, women's studies, or any other program where 95 percent of your classmates and instructors are female.

62

Travel in Herds

If you were wondering why none of the girls from your bowling club ever get hit on during ladies night—don't worry, it's not that you are lacking in personal charms. It's just that the mooks down at the end of the bar find the sight of thirty-seven women in matching pink and black bowling shirts a little daunting. All your female bonding is actually reinforcing their greatest fear: that women really don't need them at all. Unless one of you becomes weak and wanders away from the herd, all thirty-seven of you are going to stay single forever.

Of course if your uniforms consisted of fringed go-go boots and ten-gallon hats, that would be another story altogether. No one finds the Dallas Cowboy Cheerleaders intimidating.

63

Use Unconvincing Dirty Talk

It's three A.M., his place. The lighting is low and reddish. The music of Prince plays softly from the CD player. You emerge from the bathroom in a black leather corset and a pair of six-inch spike heels. His eyes glow with a lascivious passion as he kicks off his motorcycle boots and makes his way toward you. As the two of you fall backward onto his gently undulating water bed he suddenly cries out, "Talk dirty to me baby!"

While the words "Oh yes, yes! Touch my . . . my . . . you know what . . . with your big fat . . . Golly!" may not turn him on, they may help you stay single forever.

64

Have a Chaw

While many men will pretend to be open-minded on the subject of women and chewing tobacco, a double standard still operates: No matter how much they profess to admire the size of Wade Boggs' chaw, when push comes to shove no man wants to make babies with a woman who squirts black juice into a beer can in public. A pinch between your cheek and gums is therefore not only a pleasant and legal high, but an effective, if somewhat drastic, means of staying single forever.

65

Stuffed Animals—And the Women Who Love Them

Once the campy novelty of making love to an adult woman under the frozen gaze of a hundred pairs of bunny rabbit eyes has worn off, most men find stuffed animals to be a big sexual turnoff. The truth is that past the age of twenty there are only two legitimate excuses for excessive female stuffed animal ownership: 1) You are a reformed drug addict serving a ten-year sentence in a federal penitentiary for armed robbery; or, 2) You are mentally handicapped. Since your value as a sexual *objet* will not be enhanced by a resemblance to either of these two groups, a vast Snoopy collection may be an important tool in your continued pursuit of singledom.

66

Become a Thrill Seeker

There must be some variety in life—not everyone is meant to be as processed as a lump of Velveeta cheese. If your self-destructive streak has long been the talk of your family and friends my advice is—forget the therapist. Act on your impulses. The more dangerous and outlandish the liaison, the less likely it will be that you will wake up ten years down the line, dandling a rosy-cheeked baby on your knee, a prisoner in a split-level on Long Island. So go ahead—follow your bliss—even if he's your sister's husband.

67

Be a Closet Lesbian

Another fine way of remaining single is by being a closet lesbian, deeply in denial about your sexual orientation. If you have no interest in men romantically speaking, you'll undoubtedly send out messages that you're unavailable. Meanwhile, remaining closeted ensures that no nice women are going to sweep you off your feet either. Therefore, with one simple twist of your rigid psyche, you have increased your chances for singledom twofold.

Do yourself a favor, however, and stay away from politics on any level. With your standoffishness (not to mention your excellent tennis game) you'd make a fabulous First Lady . . .

68

Read Him Your Poetry

Shy men prefer a feisty wench,
Bold guys go for helpless damsels.
Pacifists may secretly adore
Pistol-toting mam'sls.

A bodybuilding thug may think
Your glutes are the cat's pajamas.
Even Buddhist monks will flirt
With Dalai Lama mamas.

There are lots of men in this big wide world,
From Catalan to Istanbul,
But they'll all avoid you like the plague,
If you're a poetry-writing fool.

(continued)

The poetry-writing fool has odes
For every hour of the day,
And when out on a date she'll recite them all
At the drop of a beret.

When he listens to her versify,
A man's mind will go numb with fear,
As he silently prays she can't play the bongos,
And wishes he were drinking a beer.

So if your wish is to avoid romance
And stay forever single,
Don't be shy about trying out
Your newest rhyming jingle.

69

Overdress

When it comes to overdressing in order to keep potential suitors at bay, few women could rival the chops of the character of Norma Desmond in the movie *Sunset Boulevard*—but don't take my word for it. Next time you're invited to a Fourth of July picnic with your new beau try putting on a moth-eaten mink coat, two inches of pancake makeup, and a diamond tiara. By the time you smile and say "Ready for my close-up, Mr. DeMille!" he'll probably already have his deposit back from the rental car.

70

Love Me, Love My Akita

While you may love Fido for his playful spirit, his loyal soul, and his long furry nose, few men will find the sight of a 150-pound Akita growling at them from the foot of the bed to be a big turn-on. By refusing to lock this beast in the bathroom during sex not only are you severely imperiling your lover's ability to father children, but you are also allowing a dog to decide your romantic future.

What a good idea. To paraphrase Charlie the Tuna, Akitas don't like men with good taste: They like men who taste good.

71

Have a Father Complex

If you think it's sweet that Daddy still calls you those funny nick-names, love the feel of his scratchy beard against your face, and are secretly thrilled when someone mistakes you for his wife, then I have some good news, Princess. A father complex is a great way to stay single forever. The reason why is that any man with half a brain in his head will recognize your relationship with Dad for what it is—a romance. Unless he's a glutton for punishment, he'll soon be off in search of greener pastures.

Fortunately, that won't bother you one bit. After all, you've already found the relationship you're looking for.

72

Buy In-line Skates

You first noticed them in the park on Saturday mornings: the legion of lithe, Lycra-clad thirty-somethings gliding gracefully through the crowd. You commented to yourself on the high percentage of apparently single men among their ranks. At the time it seemed like a great way to meet guys while keeping fit. Now you find yourself wondering—is in-line skating really for me?

Too bad you didn't ask that question before you put on those Rollerblades® and found yourself careening down the street at seventy miles per hour, directly into oncoming traffic.

73

Spend the Weekend at Your Parents'

For some women, the concept of a life of uninterrupted singledom just isn't satisfying enough: They also need the thrill of feeling as if *they will never have another date again as long as they live.* This is best accomplished by spending every weekend at your parents' home in the burbs, lying on the floor of the family room watching TV (remember—extra points for *Partridge Family* reruns!). Now that's life on the edge.

74

Be a Victim ... Or Just Look Like One!

While the true victim has an uncanny knack for attracting the unlovable, destructive partners that so many committed singles would kill for, she may also have an unfortunate tendency to spend years in relationships with them. The best way, then, to enjoy the benefits of victimhood is not actually to be a victim, but just to look like one. With this in mind, the recipe for the standard biker-chick victim is as follows: acid-washed jeans, Harley-Davidson tattoo, souvenir T-shirts from Daytona Beach (fringe is preferable), grown-out bleach job/perm, and menthol cigarettes.

It may be a little difficult to explain to your partners at the law firm at first, but in the long run, you're worth it!

75

Get Depressed

In discussing singleness and depression, it's often difficult to say which came first, the chicken or the egg. As in certain advanced cases of singleness, depressed people often generally lack the energy to pursue romantic relationships and rarely get out on Friday nights. Fortunately, through a combination of therapy and prescription drugs, clinical depression is now largely treatable.

Then again, why mess with greatness? You may not be a lot of laughs but you will stay single forever.

76

Be a Lousy Cook

If you've never even been able to bake a potato successfully, going out on a limb to impress a man by whipping up a complicated meal is a big mistake. Men have a sixth sense about these things: They can tell when a woman is only acting domestic in order to ensnare them. Not only that, if he's in the least bit litigiously inclined you're going to have a lawsuit on your hands. FYI—pork is not meant to be served rare.

77

Win at Scrabble

The male ego is a delicate thing. That's why a woman who gets stuck with the letters Y, G, M, Z, R, Y, and U and immediately spells out "ZYMURGY" (the chemistry of fermentation, as applied in brewing) will usually stay single forever.

78

Be a Bitch

Courtship behavior among the great crested grebe consists of twelve distinct phases: 1) the discovery phase, in which one bird approaches the other; 2) the preening phase, where each bird flicks its feathers at the other; 3) the display phase, where both birds assume the ghostly "penguin" pose; 4) the weed phase, in which a water weed is carried and presented by each bird to the other; 5) the . . .

"Screw the birds!" screeches the testy single. "What the hell has this got to do with the fact that I'm still single?"

More than you think, sweetheart.

79

Have an In-Bed Identity Crisis

In an ideal world many men would like to believe that their sexual prowess will rock your world. Barring that, most of them will gladly settle for someone who is paying attention. A woman who is involved in an in-bed identity crisis falls into neither category: hence, another fine way of staying single forever. With all the rolling around that goes on during lovemaking, however, it's sometimes difficult to find the time for a full-scale angst attack. For this reason we have developed a convenient shorthand for a tortured inner monologue that is guaranteed to alienate even the most insensitive suitor. The next time you're in bed with someone, sigh heavily and try one of these lust stoppers:

What am I doing here?

Who am I?

God I'm so fucked up.

God I'm so confused.

God I'm so—never mind.

80

Be a Lurker

Lurking, for those who are unfamiliar with the term, is when a woman spends weeks, even months, of her time prowling the side streets of an unfamiliar neighborhood, in the hopes that she will "casually bump into" the man about whom she is obsessing. Like her cousin the stalker, the lurker has low self-esteem and a compulsive personality; however, the lurker is never dangerous. In fact, if a "chance meeting" ever does occur between herself and the object of her desire, the nail-biting lurker will only stammer incoherently and gaze at her feet with the glassy-eyed panic of a deer caught in the headlights of an oncoming car.

Thus we have touched on the paradox that makes lurking such an effective means of remaining single forever: Despite all her efforts, she can never think of anything to say.

81

Get Religion

Woman does not live by bread alone: Just as she has emotional and physical needs, she also has spiritual ones. Like Anthony Quinn looking up and noticing the stars for the first time at the end of Fellini's *La Strada*, whether we like it or not, all of us are part of a reality that is larger than ourselves. Whether you do Buddhist chanting, handle rattlesnakes, or simply take time out once in a while to commune with nature in a loving way, developing a spiritual practice is a wonderful way to lead a fuller life.

Turning your spiritual practice into a date is also a wonderful way of staying single forever, particularly if the man you're seeing is a lapsed Catholic. True, he may be impressed by your devotion to the Virgin Mary when you prostrate yourself, weeping at the feet of the Blessed Mother, but he's definitely going to stop wondering what you'd look like in a garter belt.

82

Only Sleep with Old Friends

No matter what's going on in your life, you know you can always turn to your old pal George—and vice versa. Since senior year of high school you've seen each other through twenty-seven romances and one marriage. Now that you're both single again, you've started talking about whether or not the two of you should try sleeping together. Even though he's all for it, you have to admit you've never had much feeling for George, physically. But then again sexual attraction isn't everything, is it?

No, of course not. But it will seem like everything when old Georgie is lying on top of you, dripping with sweat and moaning "Do me baby" in your ear. Tomorrow over coffee when you're seeing the angry, rejected side of George for the first time, you'll realize that not only is sleeping with friends a great way to stay single forever, it can also really screw up your life but good.

83

Blow Off the Wrong Guy

The next time you're invited to brunch in a fancy town house on the Upper East Side, do everything you can to ignore the yuppie wannabe who's trying to strike up a conversation with you. Pay no attention when he natters on about the family compound down in Palm Beach. Snicker to yourself when he mentions the name of the new publishing venture he's trying to get off the ground—who ever heard of a magazine called *George*? When he obliquely refers to "my late father, the President," assume that he is lying in order to impress you. After the party when he walks you out of the building and hints that he might like to see you again, make sure you don't give him your phone number or offer to share a cab downtown. Later on when your friends say "Do you know who that was?" the full ramifications of your tactical error will set in.

What can I say? Another great way to stay single forever.

84

Be a Jock

As children, boys and girls differ greatly in the ways in which they play. While girls may prefer to experiment with role-playing, boys are more likely to establish a pecking order among themselves by engaging in highly structured, competitive games. In many males, these competitive feelings often persist into adult life, where business deals can be worked out on the squash court or on the softball field. While they may profess to be unconcerned with the outcome of these casual sporting events, victory is still cause for celebration, while defeat can be a crushing blow to the ego.

Especially if the person who just beat the pants off him in basketball is the woman he's dating. As long as you've got the chops—another fine way of staying single forever.

85

Practice Tantric Sex (Until You Get It Right)

While you may win brownie points for creativity, dabbling in the ancient practice of tantric sex can also greatly increase your chances of eternal singledom. Although tantric sex is rumored to be a great stress reliever that can help bring both partners to heightened levels of intimacy and sexual awareness, in actuality few things are guaranteed to raise a man's blood pressure than the sight of a naked woman glimpsed from between his painfully inverted thighs (the *makala* or *crocodile* pose) as she desperately thumbs through a copy of *The Joy of Tantric Sex* searching for a way to get him out of the *asana* without spraining anything.

Please note: When practicing tantric sex, never discount the possibility that you are holding the book upside down.

86

Work on Your Self-Esteem

As any psychotherapist, social worker, and Psychic Friends' Network counselor knows, having a precarious sense of self is a big stumbling block to healthy interpersonal relationships. Fortunately, most chronic singles grew up in environments that encouraged exactly this lack of self-esteem. However, if you have always been on solid ground romantically speaking, you may need to work on your self-esteem. Try putting ten minutes of quiet time aside every day to tell yourself what a despicable, unlovable worm you are. It's high time you replaced those old, positive tapes with new, negative ones.

87

Correct His Grammar

If a woman chides a man over his use of the double negative on the first date, he'll be irked but he'll still find her attractive. A gentle reminder about splitting his infinitive on the second date and there will be a mole on her cheek he hadn't noticed before. An in-depth lecture about the dangers of a dangling participle on the third date may cause him to remark to himself about the luxuriousness of her mustache. But it's not until the fourth date (if there is one) that the transformation will be complete. That's when he'll realize that for the last two weeks he has been drinking margaritas with Elsa Grof, his sixth-grade English teacher.

So if you want to stay single go ahead and say "Never use a preposition to end a sentence with!"

88

Too Much Perfume

Intimacy is a difficult thing. Many of us put up walls without knowing it. We create barriers between ourselves and the outside world, men especially. Maybe we've been hurt before. Maybe we feel inadequate and are trying to compensate. Whatever the reason the choice always seems to be the same: Let the wall down and risk being hurt, or leave the wall up and stay single forever.

Now would you do me a favor and sit over there? All that Tea Rose perfume you're wearing is making my eyes water.

89

Don't Laugh at His Jokes

While you may regard a relationship as serious business that is not to be taken lightly, keep in mind that nothing is quite so dismaying to a potential swain as a woman who greets his joke about a five-hundred-pound gorilla with stony silence. But don't worry— by continuing to respond to his attempts at humor with a frozen glare and the words "I'm sorry, but I just don't . . ." not only are you ensuring that you will stay single forever, but you're also doing the world a great service. Until you came along he was actually thinking he might pursue a career in stand-up comedy.

90

Surprise Him with a Threesome

It's a well-known fact that many men have fantasies about having sex with two women at once. Few people realize that tapping into this fantasy life is also a fun and adventurous way of staying single forever. The trick lies in not letting your date know what you have up your sleeve. Imagine his surprise when, after a romantic dinner for two at your place, "Linda" appears in a garter belt and hose and cozies up between the two of you on the couch. If he doesn't respond immediately, drop a hint that the two of you are blood relations. He'll be out the door before you can say *ménage à trois*. Please note: This plan may backfire if he's an extremely horny eighteen-year-old or has his own television ministry.

91

Throw a Dinner Party

While Edith Wharton would disagree, throwing a dinner party can be a great way of ensuring that you do not hook up with that eligible young bachelor who's new in town. You must, however, follow these steps: 1) Make sure you invite seventeen other people so you'll be completely stressed when he arrives promptly at seven-thirty; 2) Seat him between yourself and your best female friend who is also single; 3) Challenge yourself by creating a meal that is well beyond your capabilities as a chef so that the guy and your friend will have something to bond about while you're running back and forth in the kitchen in desperation.

Although you may stay single forever, next year when you're giving the toast at their wedding, the line about your lasagna is going to get a very big laugh.

92

Jump the Gun

Whether it's the subtly inappropriate use of the pronoun "we" in conversation, or a tendency to speculate wildly about what your children will look like, nothing ensures that you will never see a man again like the tendency to jump the gun on a first date. So if you want to stay single forever, lift your glass, look him straight in the eye, and say, "Baby, I got big plans for us!"

93

Be Obsessively Clean

While the obsessively clean, anal-retentive woman may remain single forever, it would be sexist to think that it's because all men are slobs. Actually, there are a lot of men out there who shower before and after sex, fold their pants when undressing for bed, and share her dislike for germ-laden bodily fluids. The only problem is they're more interested in each other than they are in her.

94

Be a Slob

Eight P.M. Your place. The music is hard-core, the lighting is subterranean. He unknots his sweaty bandanna and flings it toward the pile of dirty laundry that towers above you. As he makes his way through the obstacle course that is your bedroom, fear blazes in his eyes—the fear that he's about to step on something that is alive. Gathering you in his arms he murmurs, "Why don't you slip into something more comfortable while I wait right here?" Moments later you emerge from the bathroom wearing a pair of dirty sweatpants and a torn brassiere and . . .

Hey! Where did he go?

95

Ask Him to Co-sign a Loan

Asking a man to co-sign a loan is a great way to stay single forever, particularly if you bring all the paperwork along with you on a date. Get him drunk, butter him up, put your hand on his thigh under the table. When he's completely woozy with wine and lust, whip out your loan forms, and try to get him to sign on the dotted line, three copies in triplicate. If he doesn't sober up fast, for God's sake, try to get his watch. A mark like that doesn't come along every day!

96

Tell Him Your Dreams

While you may think that the dream you had last night about a truckload of purple bananas was really cute, telling a man about it is a great way to stay single forever. Many of the men you will date expect the persistently single woman to have a tendency toward this kind of self-involvement; an uninvited peek at your subconscious, however, is not the big turnoff here.

The turnoff is, he was driving the truck.

97

Create a Scene

While dating someone presents a myriad of opportunities for an inventive single woman to create a scene, in our minds the classics are still the best. Thus within the rather broad category of Scene Creation, we highly recommend "Getting Dead Drunk at a Family Function." Unlike "Throwing a Glass of Wine in His Face at a Restaurant," which will only momentarily involve a bunch of strangers at surrounding tables, this classic eyebrow-raiser offers the single woman the opportunity to include her date's entire family in her little melodrama.

Please note: Before "Getting Dead Drunk at a Family Function," it's best to conduct an informal sociological study of his immediate family. If they hail from the former Soviet Union or are of WASP descent, you will probably fit right in.

98

Get Along Great with His Mother

While there is no logical reason why hitting it off with a man's mother will cause him so much displeasure, the fact remains that excessive cross-generational female bonding may be one of the factors that lead to eternal singleness. No matter how strong the mother-child bond is, in adult life most men regard their mothers with a combination of guilt and annoyance. A woman who spends an hour a day on the phone with his mom, therefore, will begin to associate herself with these guilty, irritated feelings, particularly if she begins to voice the opinion that he's wasting his life playing the bass and should really think about going back to medical school.

99

Practice Heavy-handed Feminism

"I want you to know that this entry isn't funny at all. Every day all over the globe people are being tortured and mutilated—and for what? Because they're women. Ever hear of a clitoridectomy? Oh, go ahead, snicker. No doubt the suffering of millions of women is a big joke to you. After all, you've bought into the existing white male culture, hook, line, and sinker. That's what all this talk about 'staying single forever' is about. Let me tell you, I'm not about to mutilate myself for your corrupt value system. I'M NOT SHAVING MY LEGS FOR ANY MAN."

When was the last time anyone asked you?

100

Be a Pessimist

If it isn't clear to you by now that having a rotten, negative attitude about romance greatly increases your chances of remaining single forever, go back and begin this book again, paying special attention to items 1 to 99. If your glass still looks half-full, rather than half-empty, call your doctor immediately. Your daily dosage of Prozac may need to be adjusted.

101

Write a Book on How to Stay Single Forever

Writing a book on how to stay single forever is like walking through a field in the middle of a thunderstorm holding a lightning rod over your head—you're basically asking to get hit by lightning. And if this doesn't work, nothing will!

About the Author

Jenny Lombard is a playwright, and has had her work produced in New York by the Atlantic Theater Company, the Ensemble Studio Theatre, and Alice's Fourth Floor Theatre. She has also worked as a comedy writer for Nickelodeon and Comedy Central, and as a screenwriter. She is a practicing single until she gets it right.